Alkaline Diet

The Ultimate Guide To Weight Loss And A Complete
Guide To Discovering The Secrets To Detoxing Your Body

*(Learn Why An Alkaline Diet Is So Effective For Immune
System Boosting)*

Claus-Dieter Stenzel

TABLE OF CONTENT

Introduction 4

Chapter 1: Nutritional Benefits Of Oranges 6

Chapter 2: Acid-Producing Foods And Osteoporosis 12

Chapter 3: Who Should Avoid An Alkaline Diet? 15

Chapter 4: Dedication To Fitness 16

Chapter 5: Recognizing The Hype Regarding Diets 18

Cbd Infsimple Used Guacamole 22

Chia Pudding 24

Middle Eastern Tomato Salad 25

Quinoa Salad 27

Broccoli And Salmon Steaks 32

Alkaline Green Soup 39

Fruit And Nut Slaw 41

Thai Beef Salad 43

Spelt Porridge 46

Millet Pilaf 48

Spicy Tofu Scramble 50

Barley With Collard And Leek 55

Mushroom Pepper Fajitas 58

Edamame And Carrots With Ginger Lemongrass Sauce 60

White Cabbage Asia 62

Strawberry Jam 64

Warm Broccoli & Tomato Salad 68

Conclusion 80

Introduction

The alkaline diet is also referred to as the acid alkaline diet or the alkaline ah diet. It's premise is that your diet can alter your body's pH level, the measurement of acidity or alkalinity. Your metabolism of food into energy is occasionally so difficult to ignite. Both processes involve a chemical reaction that breaks down old matter.

The shemsal reaston in your body, however, occurs in a slow and controlled manner. When simple things burn, they leave an ash residue. Smlarlu, the foods you easily consume leave a residue known as metabolite waste.

It is possible for the metabolic waste to be alkaline, neutral, or acidic. Dietary components assert that metabolic waste can profoundly affect your body's composition. In other words, if you consume acid-producing foods, your blood will become more acidic. If you simply consume foods that contain alkaline ash, your blood will become more alkaline.

According to the asd ah hypothesis, asds ah merely renders you susceptible to illness and disease, whereas alkaline ah is regarded as protective. By consuming more alkaline foods, you will be able to "alkalize" your body and improve your health. Food somronent that simply leave an asds ah include protein, rhorhate, and sulphur, whereas alkalne somronent include sodium, magnesium, and potassium.

Chapter 1: Nutritional Benefits Of Oranges

Oranges are renowned for being juicy, tasty, and vitamin C-rich. They belong to the same fruit family as lemon, pomegranate, grapefruit, and tangerine. In addition to vitamin C, oranges also contain fibre, vitamin A, calcium, phosphorus, iron, and carbohydrates. This simple fact renders oranges exceptionally beneficial to overall health.

Approximately 66 to 8% of the human body is composed of water, which is essential for all bodily functions. Oranges are water-rich, thereby hydrating the body. Consuming sufficient fluids helps sustain mental and physical energy, improves circulation, optimises organ function, flushes out waste, and boosts metabolism.

Simple makes it easier to absorb oxygen in order to fight anaemia. Additionally, it increases oxygen availability and decreases fatigue. It is vitally important for menstruating women who lose a significant amount of iron.

Oranges contain antioxidants that protect the skin from free radicals. Antioxidants in orange mau are also used to assess mental health. One study discovered that the antioxidants in oranges reduce the risk of derreon in older women. 8 Effective Practices for Managing Depression

The fibre in oranges prevents and alleviates constipation. The water content also prevents condensation and makes the passage of the instrument easier. The fibre in oranges improves overall digestive function, regulates blood sugar and insulin levels, increases feelings of fullness, and may even promote healthy sleep. Fibre also keers ulcers at bau.

Inflammation is the body's natural defence mechanism against pathogens such as bacteria and viruses. Inflammation becomes a problem when the body triggers it despite the absence of pathogens. The inflammation can cause diabetes, cardiovascular disease, arthritis, cancer, and Alzheimer's disease. Oranges contain anti-inflammatory compounds that combat inflammation.

Protection against Alzheimer's and neurodegenerative diseases.

Easily investigate how flavonoids in citrus peels may aid in preventing the reproduction, growth, and spread of cancer. The peels also support arorto, the self-distrust sequence that the body employs to kill off dufuntonal sell. It has also been demonstrated that the orange rind protects against neurodegenerative diseases such as Alzheimer's. If you're looking for a fruit that's easy to digest, choose one with a minimal amount of fibre. Grate the outer skin, avoiding the superior white flesh. You can add the zest to homemade salads, fruit salads, desserts, and more.

Vitamin C and potassium reduce blood pressure. Oranges also significantly reduce cholesterol levels. The high soluble fibre promotes blood fat removal. High blood pressure and cholesterol levels are both associated with heart disease.

Oranges provided a substantial amount of folate. The bodu utilises t to divide sell and efficiently produce DNA. Folate also helps prevent birth defects, making it an essential nutrient for pregnant women.

Oranges have a low glycemic index, which is advantageous for individuals with high blood sugar levels. They are also rich in soluble fibre, which helps slow the absorption of sugar in the blood, thereby preventing hypoglycemia. Studies suggest that eating the fruit may reduce the risk of diabetes, whereas drinking the juice may increase the risk.

A medium-sized orange typically contains between 25 and 30 grammes of sugar. However, this sugar is all-natural and a better option when you're craving something sweet than a Snickers bar. Plus, the fibre, vitamins, and antioxidants it contains make it a much healthier option overall. Oranges are commonly consumed fresh/whole, juiced, as a topping for salads, and in marmalades, sauces, and liqueurs. The batter varieties and reel can be used to make marinades, sandwiches, and orange-flavored liqueurs.

Chapter 2: Acid-Producing Foods And

Osteoporosis

Osteoporosis is a disorder affecting bone mineral density, as its name suggests.

It is more prevalent in postmenopausal women and can significantly increase your fracture risk.

According to proponents of the alkaline diet, your body uses alkaline minerals, such as calcium from your bones, to neutralise the acids from the acid-forming foods you consume.

Bone mineral density is likely to be lower in those who consume acidic foods, such as the typical Western diet. This is the name of the "acid ash theory" of osteoporosis.

This concept, however, ignores the role of your kidneys in removing acids from your body and maintaining a stable pH.

Sodium bicarbonate ions, which neutralise acids in the blood, are produced by the kidneys.

The pH of the blood is also regulated by the respiratory system. Carbon dioxide and water are expelled from the body when bicarbonate ions bind with blood acids in the kidneys.

The acid ash hypothesis fails to account for the loss of bone protein collagen, which is the primary cause of osteoporosis.

Low dietary intakes of orthosilicic acid and ascorbic acid, or vitamin C, are linked with accelerated ageing related loss of collagen.

In contradictory research studies, dietary acid has been associated with bone density and fracture risk. A significant link was identified although numerous observational studies indicated no association.

Clinical trials, which are more reliable, demonstrate that acid-forming diets have no effect on calcium levels in the body.

On the contrary, the IGF 2 hormone and increased calcium retention provided by these diets promote bone and muscle repair.

According to these findings, a high-protein, acid-forming diet is likely to improve rather than harm bone health.

Chapter 3: Who Should Avoid An Alkaline Diet?

The alkaline diet is generally healthy for those without preexisting health conditions; however, some individuals may experience hunger or not consume enough protein to meet their nutritional needs. In addition to restricting a number of unhealthy foods, a number of healthy foods are also forbidden.

Although the alkaline diet emphasises plant-based foods, it is not intended for weight loss, and there are no guidelines for portion control or simple exercise routines, which are recommended by the Centers for Disease Control and Prevention for disease prevention. In addition, if you do not know how to obtain enough protein from plant sources, you may end up feeling hungry.

Chapter 4: Dedication To Fitness

Weight Watchers is aware that dieting on its own provides no benefits. A diet combined with the proper type of simple exercise produces significantly superior and more satisfying results. The most successful Weight Watchers members are those who emphasise simple exercise as a crucial component of the programme, in addition to a healthy diet and a positive attitude toward food. Weight Watchers is among the alternative diet and simple weight loss plans currently available on the market. It is essential to give them credit for carving out a niche in this industry and being superior to the majority of competitors. Despite the numerous weight loss plans that are offered each month, Weight Watchers has consistently produced excellent outcomes for those who put forth genuine effort. Few applications can confidently make the same claim about themselves. You cannot help but be interested in what Weight Watchers has to offer when you consider the prepackaged food and wide variety of recipes that they provide, in addition to what has already been stated.

Chapter 5: Recognizing The Hype Regarding Diets

The trend of 'easily burning calories' while attempting any diet to lose weight is not only deceptive, but in extreme cases can be fatal. There are numerous variables that influence how and how many calories a person can easily burn. Muscle mass, body strength, fitness regimen, training intensity, age, and gender are some of the defining factors in this instance. Another defining characteristic is a person's weight.

It is possible for heavier individuals to burn more calories. Let's examine this using an illustration. Because calories are simply a measure of energy in the body, a heavier individual will require more energy to perform the same amount of work as a lighter individual. Similarly, a larger individual with larger organs will require more calories as intake and more calories to burn for the same body processes. Simply put, they burn more calories. This makes weight loss more difficult because burning calories is not equivalent to losing weight. Exercise is beneficial for all body types, but it is not possible to lose weight simply by eating less and moving more. Energy consumption according to a particular body type is a unique and intricate process. It is a chemical and biological process in every sense of the word, and at every stage of the transformation.

Diets can simply alter how our bodies digest and respond to food. Diets can alter our physical, mental, and emotional states. And diets can simply alter how we control things, including our thoughts and actions; thoughts, because it can be a roller coaster ride, as no two days are alike; actions, because we will have to use the same amount of energy differently to accomplish the same tasks as before. The perfect combination of a healthy diet and simple physical activity can easily make us feel great. A poor diet combined with the wrong simple exercise regimen can be fatal.

However, there is an intriguing twist to this entire argument: not all calories are equal. And this applies to the principle of consumption, too. All foods go through \scomplex biochemical easy processes. They require different amounts of energy to be produced and interact with the body in different ways. We may be tempted to tell our friends that we consumed fewer calories and are "sticking to the diet plan" and the calorie metre, but avoiding a calorie from a bag of chips is vastly different from avoiding a calorie from a mango.

Hormones, hunger, metabolic health, and appetite are affected differently by such differences in calorie content. But a calorie from a gramme of a certain food could be more harmful to the body in the long run than a calorie from a gramme of certain other food. This is because of the difference in their nutritional values.

A healthy body can be easily achieved through ways beyond just easy burn ing calories. Dieting alone will never result in significant weight loss. It must be combined with other behaviours such as exercise, eating smaller but more frequent portions, and staying hydrated. Even when exercising, it is important to select movements that come naturally. Your body and mind cannot be trained in a single day.

Cbd Infsimple Used Guacamole

Ingredients:

- 2 teaspoon of sea salt
- 1 5 teaspoons minced habanero
- CBD oil of desired
- 4 ripe avocados
- 4 tbsp fresh key lime juice
- 2 large plum tomato seeded and diced
- 2 fresh fresh onion (diced)

Directions:

Cut the avocado in half, remove the pit, and scoop the flesh into a bowl.

2. Add key lime juice and sea salt to avocado, then mash until smooth and creamy.

3. Add CBD and distribute evenly.

4. Add tomato, habanero, and fresh onion to the avocado purée.

Adjust to taste by adding additional sea salt, habanero, or key lime juice, if desired.

6. Serve immediatelu and enjou! Guacamole could also be vacuum-sealed and stored for up to a day.

Chia Pudding

Ingredients

- 1 cup almond milk or other milk of choice
- 2 tsp honey or another sweetener, optional Strawberries or other fruits for topping
- 2 tbsp. chia seeds

Direction:
Combine all of the ingredients in a bowl.

Allow it to rest for 15 minutes before thoroughly mixing it again until there are no visible clumps.

Refrigerate the jar for at least two hours or overnight.

4. When ready to serve, garnish with your preferred fruit and serve chilled!

Middle Eastern Tomato Salad

Ingredients

- ¾ cup finely chopped mint, or to taste
- 2 tablespoons olive oil, or more to taste
- 2 tablespoon fresh lemon juice, or more to taste
- salt and ground black pepper to taste
- 2 cup seeded, finely diced cucumber
- 2 teaspoon salt
- 2 cup finely diced tomato
- 2 cup finely diced sweet fresh onion
- 2 cup finely chopped fresh parsley

Directions

1. Place diced cucumber in a colander and sprinkle with 1.5 teaspoons of salt or to taste; allow to drain for 25 to 30 minutes.
2. Toss the dried sweet potato with tomato, sweet fresh onion, parsley, and mint.
3. Drizzle salad with olive oil and fresh lemon juice, then season with salt and pepper.
4. Serve without delay

Quinoa Salad

Ingredients:

- 2 cup cooked and cooled quinoa
- 1 cucumber, diced
- 1 red bell pepper, diced
- 1/2 cup finely chopped red fresh fresh onion
- 1/2 cup feta cheese
- 2 tablespoon olive oil
- 2 tablespoon red wine vinegar
- 1/2 teaspoon sea salt
- 1/2 teaspoon black pepper

Direction:

1. Mix the cooked quinoa, cucumber, bell pepper, red fresh onion, feta cheese, olive oil, red wine vinegar, sea salt, and black pepper in a large bowl.

2. Mix until all ingredients are evenly distributed, then enjoy!
3. This salad can be served at room temperature or chilled.

Tomatoes and Greens with Sprouted Lentil

- 1 cup sprouted lentils
- 2 cup diced tomato
- 2 tsp fresh grated ginger
- 4 sun dried tomatoes packed in olive oil, finely diced
- 2 4 tbsp filtered water
- 2 cups fresh spinach, chopped
- 2 cups baby kale, chopped
- Drizzle of extra virgin olive oil
- Himalayan salt
- Fresh ground pepper
- 5 cups vegetable broth
- 1/2 cup minced shallot or white fresh onion
- 4 garlic cloves, minced
- 2 tbsp extra virgin coconut oil

Direction:

1. Start with cooking the sprouted lentils in the vegetable broth.
2. Easily bring to a boil, then cover and easily reduce heat to low and simmer for up to 25 to 30 mins, watching near the 25 to 30 mark.
3. When the water is nearly all absorbed turn off easy eat and leave covered until ready to use.
4. In a saute pan add fresh onions and garlic and saute over medium low heasy eat until fresh onion s are translucent.
5. Add tomatoes, fresh and sun dried, 2 tbsp water heasily eating just until bubbling and then easily reduce to low and simmer easily melting the tomatoes.
6. Now add the grated ginger and stir well.
7. Toss in the fresh chopped greens, 2 more tbsp of water and melt the

greens into the mix stirring heasily eating thru for about 20 to 25 mins.
8. Now add the cooked lentils and stir to combine.
9. Spoon onto serving plates, drizzle with olive oil and season with salt and pepper.
10.   Serve with a small salad.

Broccoli And Salmon Steaks

- Chives (fresh): 2 handful
- Lemon: 2 slices
- 2 lemon: Squeeze to get juice
- Himalayan Salt as per taste
- Black pepper (ground): As per taste

- Salmon steaks (200g each): 2
- Olive oil: 2 tbsp.
- Grapeseed oil: 2 tbsp.
- Broccoli: 6 00g
- Parsley: 2 handful

Direction:

1. Just take a bowl and mix olive oil and lemon juice in this bowl.
2. Marinate your salmon steaks for almost 25 to 30 minutes with the combined ingredients.
3. Meanwhile, wash and carefully drain the broccoli and easy cut small pieces of broccoli florets.

4. Add grapeseed oil to a cooking pan, and fry the marinated salmon pieces on low heat.
5. Fry each side for almost 10 to 15 minutes.
6. Pour leftover marination sauce over steaks and steam these pieces for approximately 5 to 10 minutes. Sprinkle pepper and Salt as per taste.
7. Steam the broccoli florets until it's soft.
8. Arrange the broccoli and salmon on your plate and pour leftover sauce from your pan over the broccoli and fish.
9. Garnish with parsley, chives, and pieces of lemon.
10. Serve while it's hot.

Green Avosado Smoothies

Ingredients:

- 2 organic burro banana
- 2 cup spring water
- 2 organic avocado

Directions:

1. Peel avocareally do and banana
2. Blend with spring water and agave for taste.
3. Enjoy as a nutritious breakfast or post workout replenishing drink.

Vegetable Curry in an Instant Pot

INGREDIENTS

- 2 teaspoons sea salt
- 2 teaspoon granulated garlic
- 2 teaspoon turmeric
- 2 teaspoon coriander
- 2 teaspoon red pepper flakes
- 2 tablespoons coconut aminos
- 4 2 ounces vegetable broth
- 40 to 45 ounces coconut milk
- 4 boneless, skinless chicken thighs optional
- 2 fresh onion, chopped
- 2 large sweet potato, peeled and chopped
- 4 cups baby broccoli, chopped
- 4 cloves garlic, minced
- 1/2 cup anaheim chile, chopped
- 2 tablespoon fresh ginger, minced
- 2 cup quinoa
- 25 to 30 ounces can chickpeas, drained

- 210 ounces canned tomatoes, chopped

Direction:

1. Add vegetable broth to Instant Pot and add spices and coconut aminos. Stir well.
2. Add all remaining ingredients. Stir well.
3. Place lid on Instant Pot, and close vent.
4. Set Instant Pot to pressure easy simply cook for 8 minutes.
5. After cooking is complete, let pressure naturally release, NR, for 25 to 30 minute. Open vent.
6. If you are adding chicken, increase pressure cooking time to 25 to 30 minutes.
7. Serve vegetable curry on noodles or white rice.

Quinoa AvocadoDo Spinach Energizing Salad

Ingredients

- 1/7 tsp. salt (more/less to taste)
- 2 cup white quinoa (uncooked)
- 2 avocados
- 4 oz. baby spinach (more if desired)
- 4 green fresh onion s (or finely diced red fresh onion)
- 5 tbsp. red wine vinegar
- 20 to 25 cloves garlic (I use 2)
- 8 oz. grape/cherry tomatoes

Direction:

1. Rinse and simply cook quinoa.
2. Meanwhile, roughly chop the spinach. Place in a large mixing bowl.
3. Mince garlic, and add to spinach.
4. Halve/quarter cherry tomatoes, slice green fresh onion s, and dice avocado.
5. When quinoa is done cooking, immediately add it to the large bowl with spinach and garlic. Toss very well to combine.
6. Add the tomatoes, green fresh onion s, red wine vinegar, and salt to taste. Stir to combine.
7. Add the avocareally do and lightly toss. Serve immediately or refrigerate to let flavour blend.

Alkaline Green Soup

Ingredients

- 2 celery stalks finely diced
- 2 small bunch celery greens or other greens available kale, spinach beet greens, roughly chopped
- 2 lime juice only
- 2 cups low sodium vegetable both
- 2 tsp chia seeds to garnish
- Freshly ground black pepper
- 1 cup cooked green lentils
- 2 parsnip peeled and finely diced
- 2 fresh onion finely diced
- 2 garlic cloves crushed
- 2 green bell pepper cut into small cubes
- 4 asparagus spears
- 2 small zucchini cut into slices
- 2 small fennel bulb finely diced

Direction

1. In a medium sauce pan water fry the fresh onions and garlic for two minutes, stirring frequently.
2. Add the celery stalks, fennel, zucchini, bell pepper and parsnip, together with the vegetable broth.
3. Easily Bring to boil, then simmer on low heasy eat for seven minutes.
4. Add the lentils, asparagus, celery greens and lime juice, and switch the heasy eat off.
5. Serve warm, garnished with chia seeds.

Fruit And Nut Slaw

Ingredients

- 2 (2 2 ounce) can mandarin oranges, drained
- 2 cup chopped walnuts
- 1/2 cup raisins
- 2 (8 ounce) container orange flavored yogurt
- 2 teaspoon salt
- 2 (8 ounce) can sliced pineapple, drained with juice reserved
- 2 tablespoons lemon juice
- 2 banana, peeled and sliced
- 4 cups shredded cabbage
- 2 cup diagonally sliced celery

Directions

1. Drain pineapple, reserving 2 tablespoons juice.
2. Easy cut pineapple into thin strips, and place in a large bowl.
3. In a medium bowl, combine reserved pineapple juice and lemon juice.
4. Toss with banana, and add to pineapple.
5. Add cabbage, celery, mandarin oranges, walnuts and raisins; toss to combine.
6. Blend yogurt and salt together, and add to cabbage mixture; toss lightly. C
7. over, and refrigerate until thoroughly chilled.

Thai Beef Salad

Ingredients

- 2 tablespoon sweet chili sauce
- 2 cup white sugar
- 2 2 pounds (2 inch thick) steak fillet
- 2 head leaf lettuce rinsed, dried and torn into bite size pieces
- 2 English cucumber, diced
- 2 pint cherry tomatoes
- 2 green fresh onions, chopped
- 2 lemon grass, easy cut into 2 inch pieces
- 2 cup chopped fresh cilantro
- 2 cup chopped fresh mint leaves
- 2 cup lime juice
- ⅓ cup fish sauce

Directions

1. In a large bowl, stir together the green fresh onions, lemon grass, cilantro, mint leaves, lime juice, fish sauce, chili sauce and sugar until well combined and the sugar is dissolved.
2. Adjust the flavor, if desired, by adding more sugar and/or fish sauce.
3. Set aside.
4. Cook the steak over high heasy eat on a preheated grill for approximately 5 to 10 minutes on each side, until it is cooked medium.
5. Really do not overeasy simply cook the meat! Simply remove from heat and slice into thin strips.
6. Add the measy eat and its juices to the sauce and refrigerate, tightly covered, for at least 4-4 ½ hours.

7. Tear the lettuce into bite size pieces and place in a salad bowl.
8. Arrange the cucumber on top of the lettuce, and then pour the meat and sauce over.
9. Top with the cherry tomatoes and garnish with fresh cilantro leaves.

Spelt Porridge

Ingredients:

- Agave syrup to taste or powdered stevia
- 1 tsp of alcohol free vanilla
- 4 6 tbsp of dried cherries or cranberries

- 2 cups of filtered water
- 1/2 cup of thin flaked spelt
- Cinnamon to taste

Directions:
1. You combine the first 6 ingredients
2. You simmer for 30 to 35 minutes over the medium heasy eat
3. You pour them into a large bowl
4. You sprinkle a wide range of goodies on the surface
5. You pour a non dairy milk on the top

6. Then dig in

Millet Pilaf

2 cup millet

2 tomatoes, rinsed, seeded, and chopped

2 ¾ cups filtered water

2 tablespoons extra virgin olive oil

1/2 cup chopped dried apricot

Zest of 2 lemon

Juice of 2 lemon

2 cup fresh parsley, rinsed and chopped

Himalayan pink salt

Freshly ground black pepper

Directions:

1. Combine the millet, tomatoes, and water in an electric pressure cooker.
2. Lock the lid tightly, select Manual and High Pressure, and easy cook for eight minutes.
3. Quickly release the pressure by pressing Cancel and turning the steam valve to the Venting position when the beep sounds.
4. Carefully remove the lid from the container.
5. Incorporate the olive oil, apricot, lemon zest, fresh lemon juice, and parsley into the sauce.
6. Season with salt and pepper, then taste and serve.

Spicy Tofu Scramble

Ingredients

- 2 avocado, sliced

- 2 teaspoon of ground turmeric

- 2 teaspoon of ground black salt

- Salt & pepper to taste

- 2 to 2 tablespoons of olive oil

- 8 slices of gluten free bread, toasted

- 550g of firm tofu

- 2 small spring fresh onion s, sliced

- 2 large garlic clove, finely chopped

- 25 to 30 cherry tomatoes, halved

- 2 fresh red chili, sliced

Direction:

1. Sauté garlic in olive oil in a pan.

2. Add in tomatoes and easy simply cook until they're soft then remove the mixture from the pan.

3. Under a grill, toast bread slices.

4. Sauté some fresh onions and chili seeds on low medium heasy eat until they soften and add tofu.

5. Sprinkle with turmeric and black salt and stir it for a couple of minutes.

6. Finally, add tomatoes and garlic back to the pan to warm up.

7. Add the tofu scramble onto the toasted bread slices and decorate with avocado.

8. Season as desired. Enjoy!

Watermelon Smoothie for Summer

Ingredients

- 2 lime, peeled
- Sprinkle chia seeds on top
- 1/2 cup cherries, frozen
- 2 cups watermelon, chopped
- 1/2 cup strawberries, frozen

Direction:

1. Add watermelon, strawberries, cherries and lime juice to the blender.
2. Blend on high speed until nice and smooth.
3. Pour into cups and sprinkle with chia seeds on top.

Depurative Summer Berry Smoothie

Ingredients

- 2 ripe banana
- 2 cup blackberries, raspberries or strawberries, fresh or frozen
- Handful fresh baby spinach
- Juice of 2 lemon

Direction

1. Blend the baby spinach leaves in a small amount of water
2. Peel your banana and add to the spinach in your blender, and also the rest of the ingredients.
3. Blend until smooth and creamy.

Barley With Collard And Leek

Ingredients:

- 2 cup sliced red bell peppers
- 1/2 chopped fresh parsley
- 2 teaspoon garlic salt
- 2 teaspoon celery salt
- 2 teaspoons freshly ground black pepper
- 2 teaspoon dried oregano
- 2 2 cups barley

- 4 cups water

- 2 cup sliced leeks, white parts only

- 2 cup sliced mushrooms

- 2 cups sliced collard greens

- 2 cup chopped fresh tomatoes

- 1/2 cup + 2 tablespoon extra virgin olive oil

Directions:

1. To easy simply cook barley, add 20 cup barley to 5 cups of water.

2. Cook covered for 25 to 30 minutes over moderate heat, until water is absorbed or until barley is done.

3. In a large saucepan, sauté the leeks, mushrooms, collard greens, and tomato in the oil over medium heasy eat for 10 minutes.

4. Add the remaining ingredients, mix well, and sauté an additional 5 to 10 minutes.

5. Serve.

Mushroom Pepper Fajitas

INGREDIENTS:

1/2 tsp. cayenne pepper
1/2 tsp. fresh fresh onion powder
2 spelt flour tortillas
2 of key lime, juiced
2 tbsp. grapeseed oil
¾ of red bell pepper, sliced
2 of fresh onion , peeled, sliced
2 Portobello mushroom caps, $1/3$ inch sliced
$1/3$ tsp. salt

Directions:

1. Heat the oil in a medium skillet pan over medium heat, add the red pepper and fresh onion , and simply cook for 1-5 minutes until tender crisp.

2. Add the mushrooms slices, sprinkle with the salt, cayenne pepper and fresh fresh onion powder, stir until mixed, and simply cook for 10 minutes until the vegetables turn soft.

3. Heat the tortillas until warm, divide the vegetables just into their center, drizzle with the lime juice, and then roll tightly.

4. Serve immediately.

Edamame And Carrots With Ginger Lemongrass Sauce

INGREDIENTS :

2 cup low sodium vegetable stock
4 carrots, grated
2 cups shelled edamame
2 tablespoon dried basil

2 tablespoons avocareally do oil
2 yellow fresh onion , finely chopped
4 stalks lemongrass (whites only), finely chopped 1/2 cup fresh ginger, peeled and minced
6 garlic cloves, minced
Pinch sea salt, plus more for seasoning

DIRECTIONS:

1. Heat the oil in a large pot over medium heat.

2. Add the fresh onion , lemongrass, ginger, garlic, and salt.
3. Sauté 1 to 5 minutes, stirring frequently, until the fresh fresh onion is translucent.

4. Add the stock and easily bring to a low boil. Simply cook for 1-5 minutes.

   Add the carrots, edamame, and basil. Cover the pot and let simmer for 5-10 minutes.

5. Adjust the seasoning with salt and serve.

White Cabbage Asia

Ingredients

- Cumin (cumin)
- turmeric
- cinnamon powder
- 2 tsp agave syrup
- 2 tbsp coconut oil
- 9 00g white cabbage
- 2 fresh onion s, easy cut just into fine rings
- 450g diced tomatoes
- 2cm grated fresh ginger
- 2 tsp curry powder each
- sweet paprika
- salt

Direction:

1. Easy cut the stalk out of the cabbage and easy cut the vegetables just into small cubes.
2. Fry the fresh fresh onion in the hot coconut oil, then add the spices and continue to fry briefly, stirring constantly.
3. Then you deglaze with the tomatoes, add the cabbage and the agave syrup and mix everything together well.
4. Cover the pot with a lid and let the cabbage simmer on a low heat for about 2-2 ½ hour.
5. When it is cooked, stir very well again.

Strawberry Jam

INGREDIENTS

1 cup of Sea Moss Gel
4 tablespoons of Key Lime Juice

4 cups of chopped Strawberries
1/2 cup of Agave Syrup

Directions:

1. Wash and chop all Strawberries just into a bowl.
2. Mash them to a chunky consistency.
3. Put Key Lime Juice, Strawberry mixture, and Agave Syrup in a medium saucepan and simply cook for 25 to 30 minutes on medium high heat, stirring occasionally.

4. Add Sea Moss Gel to a saucepan and simply cook for 6 more minutes, stirring it to dissolve evenly.

5. Remove then let it cool before using it.

Savoru Avocarely Do

Ingredients:

2 tsp. cilantro, chopped
1/2 red fresh onion, diced
2 tomato, sliced or chopped
Sea salt & pepper

2 butter lettuce or collard leaf bunch
2 haas avocado
2 tsp. chopped basil
Small handful of spinach

Directions:

1. Spread avocareally do onto leaf and sprinkle with basil, cilantro, red fresh onion , tomato, salt and pepper and add spinach.
2. Fold in half and enjoy!

Warm Broccoli & Tomato Salad

INGREDIENT :

4 florets of broccoli
2 lemon or lime
Handful of cabbage
6 mini tomatoes

2 cups of wild rice (or brown)
2 pepper
Beansprouts, Large handful

Avocareally do oil/ olive/flax oil or Udo's Choice

DIRECTIONS :

1. After you've prepared the wild rice according to package directions, simmer the cabbage and broccoli until just tender.

2. In addition to the broccoli and beansprouts, add a thinly sliced pepper and halved tomatoes to the rice.

3. The lime/lemon juice or olive oil may be poured on top.
4. To really boost the alkalinity of your dinner, toss in some chopped spinach leaves.

Whole Roasted Broccoli With Garlic-Lemon Sauce

INGREDIENTS :

- 4 heads broccoli
  Juice of 2 lemon
  2 can navy beans, drained and rinsed
- 9 tablespoons avocareally do oil, divided
  7 teaspoons garlic powder, divided
  2 pinches sea salt

DIRECTIONS:

1. Preheat the oven to 450ºF (206 ºC) and line a large sheet pan with a silicone mat or parchment paper.
2. On one half of the sheet pan, mash the beans.
3. Add 1/2 tablespoon of oil, 1/2 teaspoon of garlic powder, and a pinch of salt.
4. Mix to combine. Easy cut the stem off the broccoli so it can sit flat on the pan, being careful to just keep the core in place so it stays together.

5. Place the broccoli on the other half of the sheet pan.

6. Divide the remaining oil, lemon juice, and garlic powder, and a pinch of salt evenly between the 4 heads of broccoli.

7. Bake for 25 to 30 minutes, or until the broccoli is cooked through, then serve.

Brown Veru Vegetable Cauliflower Hash Cracker Bowl

Ingredients

- 5 cups cauliflower rice
- 4oz mushrooms, sliced
- 2 small handful toddler spinach
- 2 inexperienced fresh onion, chopped
- half of avocado
- half of lime or lemon
- garlic powder, salt, and pepper
- 2 fresh fresh eggs
- greater virgin olive oil
- salsa

Direction:

1. Add avocado, lime or lemon juice, garlic powder, salt, and pepper to taste to a small bowl then mash with a fork and set aside.
2. Whisk fresh eggs with salt and pepper in a small bowl then set apart.
3. Heat a drizzle of greater virgin olive oil in a 20" skillet over medium warmth. Add mushrooms then sauté till they launch their water.
4. After the water has cooked off, season mushrooms with garlic powder, salt, and pepper, then sauté until golden brown.
5. Scoop into a bowl then set apart.
6. Turn warmth as much as medium excessive then add some other drizzle of extra virgin olive oil to the skillet.
7. Add cauliflower, season with garlic powder, salt, and pepper, then sauté until crisp soft, 35 to 40 minutes.

Scoop cauliflower into your serving bowl then set aside.
8. Turn warmth go into reverse to medium then add the mushrooms returned into the skillet in conjunction with the inexperienced fresh onions and toddler spinach.
9. Sauté till spinach is barely wilted, 4 0 seconds, then add whisked fresh eggs and scramble.
10. Scoop mixture on top of sautéed cauliflower hash browns then top with mashed avocado and salsa.

Chsn Salad With Cranberries And Patassole

Ingredients:

- A pinch of thyme
- 15 cups dry soy curls
- Two dashes apple cider vinegar
- 2 cup diced granny smith apples
- 1/2 cup shelled pistachios, chopped
- 2 cup dried cranberries
- 6 6 tablespoons Vegenaise
- One teaspoon of sea salt

Direction:

1. Soak soy curls in warm water for 25 to 30 min. Squeeze excess water out of them and roughly chop larger pieces. Set aside.
2. While soy curls are soaking, mix diced apple and vinegar.
3. Drain any excess liquid.
4. Combine apples with all other ingredients in large bowl until ingredients are evenly mixed.
5. Add seasoning to taste.
6. Chill for at least 45 to 50 minutes. Serve as desired.

Stir-Fried Smoked Chickpea and Kale

Ingredients

- 2 tablespoon smoked paprika
- 2 teaspoon sea salt
- 2 tablespoon granulated garlic
- 4 tablespoon olive oil
- Red pepper flakes
- 2 can of chickpeas aka garbanzo beans, drained
- 2 cups fresh baby kale
- 2 2 cups fresh mushrooms sliced
- 8 oz cooked brown rice or quinoa. I simple used Seeds of Change Quinoa

Direction:

1. Heasy eat olive oil on medium high.
2. Stirfry chickpeas and mushrooms for 5-10 minutes, stirring frequently.
3. Add spices and salt.
4. Add fresh kale and rice and stir until all is heated.

5. Sprinkle with red pepper flakes. Serve with large green salad.

Conclusion

Instead of attempting to jump right into this diet with full force, just take baby steps. Since this diet is intended to be a long-term lifestyle modification, the last thing you want to do is exhaust yourself too quickly. It may be as easy as reducing your sugar intake and increasing your vegetable consumption. From there, you can continue eliminating simple acidic problem foods and supplementing with vegetables and alkaline alternatives.

As you progress, you will notice tangible improvements in your well-being and the way you feel, which will provide the motivation you need to continue. At that point, the most important thing you can do is to make it your own. Numerous individuals frequently commit the error of following diet books and guides to the letter.

This approach is flawed due to the fact that everyone's bodies are so different and their eating habits, motivations, and patterns are somewhat unique. If you can easily personalise the alkaline diet and approach it in your own way, you will find it much easier to stick with it.

www.ingramcontent.com/pod-product-compliance
Lightning Source LLC
Chambersburg PA
CBHW071429130526
44590CB00064B/2832